Write It Right

Writing an Interview

By Cecilia Minden and Kate Roth

Published in the United States of America by
Cherry Lake Publishing
Ann Arbor, Michigan
www.cherrylakepublishing.com

Reading Adviser: Marla Conn MS, Ed., Literacy specialist, Read-Ability, Inc.
Book Designer: Felicia Macheske
Character Illustrator: Carol Herring

Photo Credits: © timyee/Shutterstock, 7; © wavebreakmedia/Shutterstock, 9, 17; © imtmphoto/Shutterstock, 11; © Creativa Images/Shutterstock, 15

Graphics Throughout: © simple surface/Shutterstock.com; © Mix3r/Shutterstock.com; © Artefficient/Shutterstock.com; © lemony/ Shutterstock.com; © Svetolk/Shutterstock.com; © EV-DA/Shutterstock.com; © briddy/Shutterstock.com; © IreneArt/Shutterstock.com

Library of Congress Cataloging-in-Publication Data has been filed and is available at catalog.loc.gov

Cherry Lake Publishing would like to acknowledge the work of The Partnership for 21st Century Skills.
Please visit *www.p21.org* for more information.

Printed in the United States of America
Corporate Graphics

Table of

CONTENTS

CHAPTER ONE

The Interview

How can you learn about other people? You can do an **interview**. You might discover something new about someone you already know!

An interview is a meeting. One person asks another person questions. The answers are written down and can be shared later with other people. How do you write an interview? First, you choose someone to interview. Then you follow these basic steps:

1. Decide what you already know.
2. Decide what you want to know.
3. Interview the person.
4. Use your notes to write up the interview.

For your first interview, pick someone you know. Maybe you would like to know more about the owner of your favorite restaurant. In this book, we'll create an example interview with a chef.

Here's what you'll need to complete the activities in this book:

- Notebook
- Pen
- Ruler
- Recording device

Asking good questions often gets you great answers.

CHAPTER TWO

Do Your Research!

Do some **research** before the interview. The chef in our example owns a restaurant. Learn about the restaurant first. What you learn may give you ideas for good questions. As you prepare, use a chart to keep track of what you already know. Let's say you know that the chef was born in Argentina. He came to the United States when he was a kid. Think about questions you may want to ask him. Does he remember living in Argentina? Did he learn to cook in Argentina?

Start your research by reading about the restaurant online.

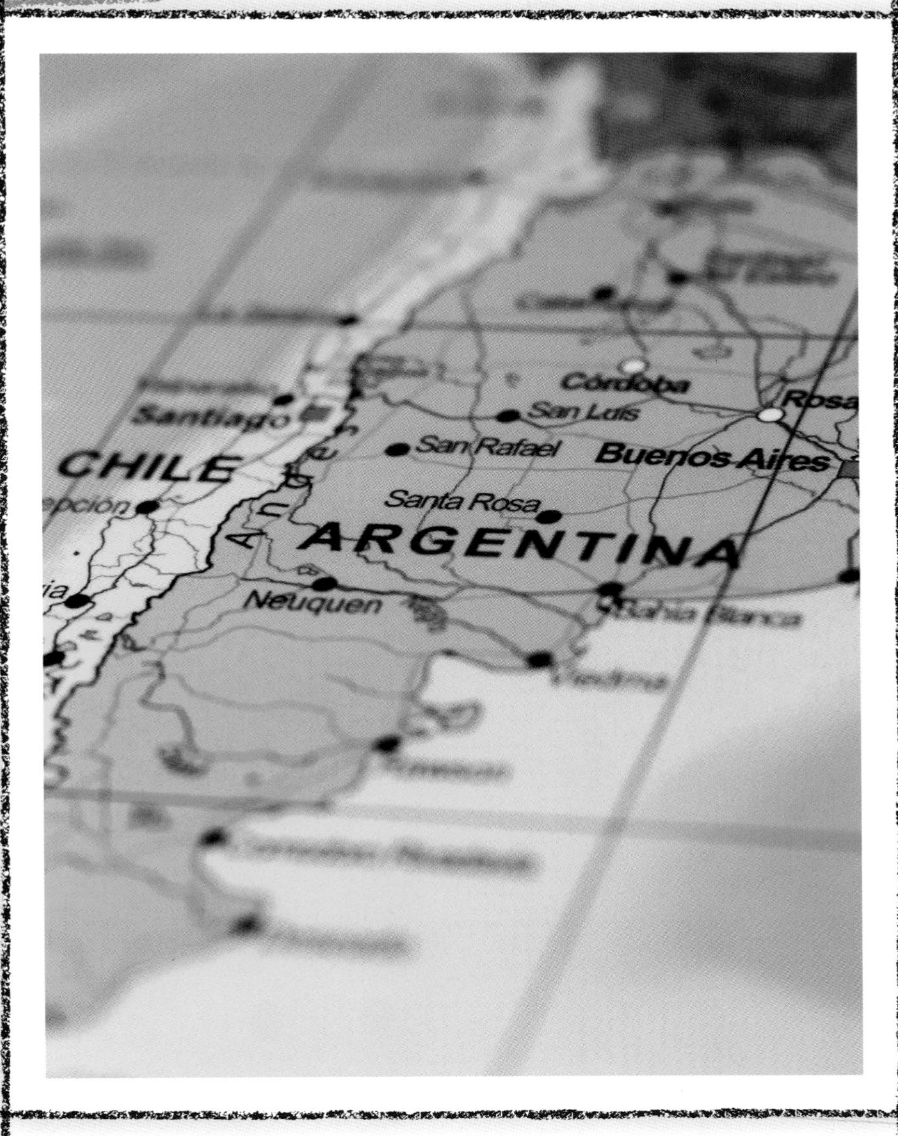

What comes to your mind when you think about Argentina?

ACTIVITY

Getting Ready

INSTRUCTIONS:

1. Use your ruler to draw a line down the center of a page in your notebook. You should now have two long boxes.
2. Write “What I Know” at the top of the box on the left.
   - In this space, write facts you know about the person you will interview. Also write what you learned from any research.
3. Write “What I Want to Know” at the top of the box on the right.
   - Think of what you want to learn from the interview. Write these things in this box.

Sample Interview Ideas

WHAT I KNOW

- His name is Lucas Romero.
- He was born in Mendoza, Argentina.
- He came to the United States when he was a kid.
- He owns a restaurant and loves to cook.

WHAT I WANT TO KNOW

- Does he remember living in Mendoza?
- What was his first impression of the United States?
- When did he know he wanted to be a chef?
- What does he like best about cooking?

CHAPTER THREE

Write Great Questions

Think of questions you will ask during the interview. Start with questions that have a yes or no answer. They are easier to answer. For example, you can ask, “Do you like to cook?” The person will answer “yes” or “no.”

You also want to ask questions that will give you more **information**. For example, ask the question, “What is it about cooking that makes you happy?” This lets the chef give you an **opinion**. He may share his reasons for preparing special dishes.

It is important to have a list of questions ready before the interview. Pay attention to the person’s answers. They can help you think of even more questions to ask.

Take the time to craft questions that will give you interesting answers.

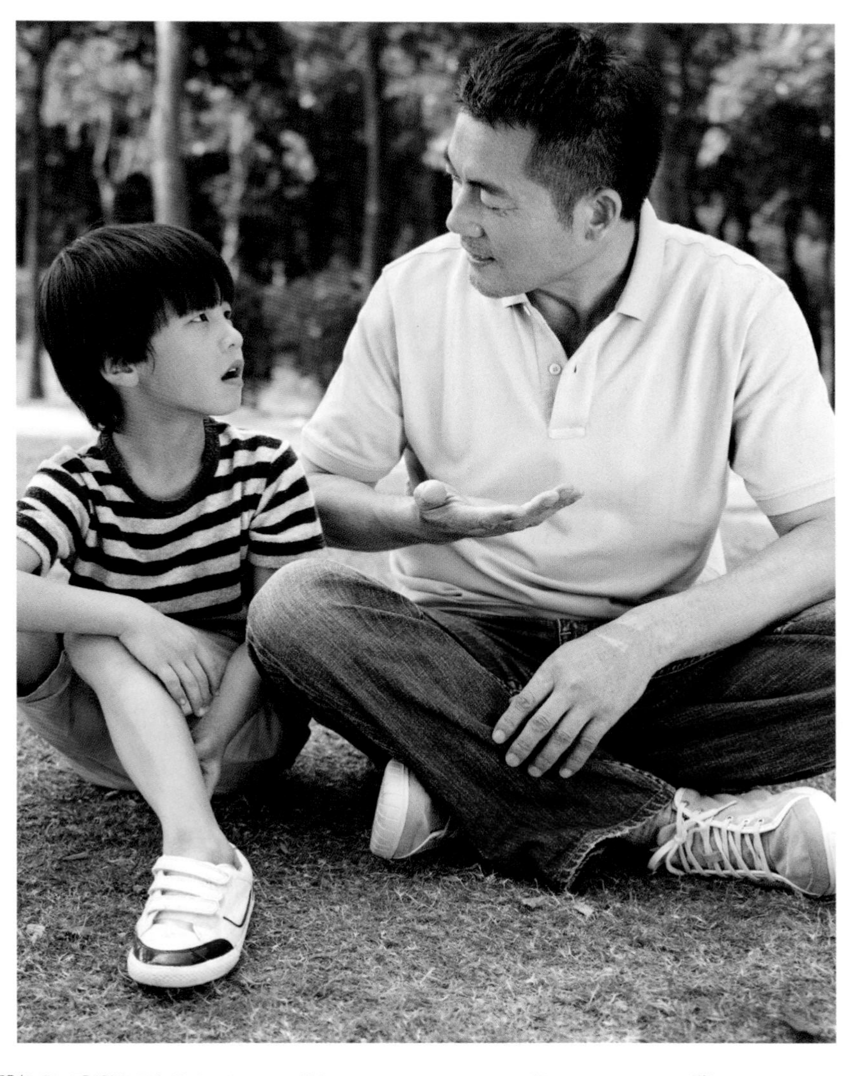

Try to ask questions that require someone to say more than "yes" or "no."

ACTIVITY

What Should You Ask?

INSTRUCTIONS:

1. Look over the chart you made earlier. Your notes will help you think of questions to ask.
2. Write the questions on another sheet in your notebook.
3. Be sure to leave space under each question for the person's answers.

Sample Interview Ideas

WHAT I KNOW

- His name is Lucas Romero.
- He was born in Mendoza, Argentina.
- He came to the United States when he was a kid.
- He owns a restaurant and loves to cook.

WHAT I WANT TO KNOW

- Does he remember living in Mendoza?
- What was his first impression of the United States?
- When did he know he wanted to be a chef?
- What does he like best about cooking?

QUESTIONS:

Q: I know you were a kid when you came to the United States. What was your first impression of the United States?
A:

Q: What made you decide to become a chef?
A:

Q: There are many wonderful dishes in Argentina. How do you choose which ones to serve in your restaurant?
A:

Q: Is there anything in particular you miss about Mendoza, Argentina?
A:

Q: Would you like to say anything else?
A:

CHAPTER FOUR

Be a Good Listener

Now it is time for the interview! It is a good idea to use a recording device during the interview. You can play the interview back later. It will help you remember details. Ask the **interviewee** for permission before recording the interview.

Ask if you may record the interview.
It will help you remember facts.

ACTIVITY

Conducting the Interview

INSTRUCTIONS:

1. Turn on the recording device if you are using one. Don't forget to turn it off after the interview.
2. Ask the questions on your list. Give the speaker time to answer each one.
3. Listen carefully. Take notes on what you want to remember about each answer. Your notes do not have to be full sentences. But they should be clear. Are you planning on using a person's exact words in part of your report? Be sure to write down those words exactly as they were spoken.
4. Look at the speaker as you take notes.
5. After the interview, thank the person for taking the time to talk with you.

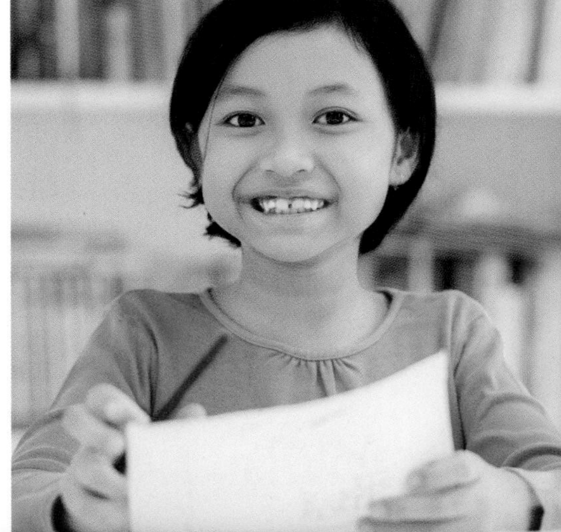

QUESTIONS:

Q: I know you were a kid when you came to the United States. What was your first impression of the United States?

A: *It was very flat! We came from a mountain city, and we moved to Texas!*

Q: What made you decide to become a chef?

A: *My mother was an excellent cook. I didn't have many friends at first. So she kept me busy in the kitchen. As I made friends, I shared some of the food I cooked. I became very popular!*

Q: There are many wonderful dishes in Argentina. How do you choose which ones to serve in your restaurant?

A: *Some are favorites that our customers expect. Some are recipes from my mother that I have changed up a bit.*

Q: Is there anything in particular you miss about Mendoza, Argentina?

A: *I miss being able to use the same ingredients. Some things are not sold here in the United States.*

Q: Would you like to say anything else?

A: *The United States and Argentina both mean a great deal to me. I am proud to be a citizen of both countries. I take pride in serving delicious dishes that cross both cultures.*

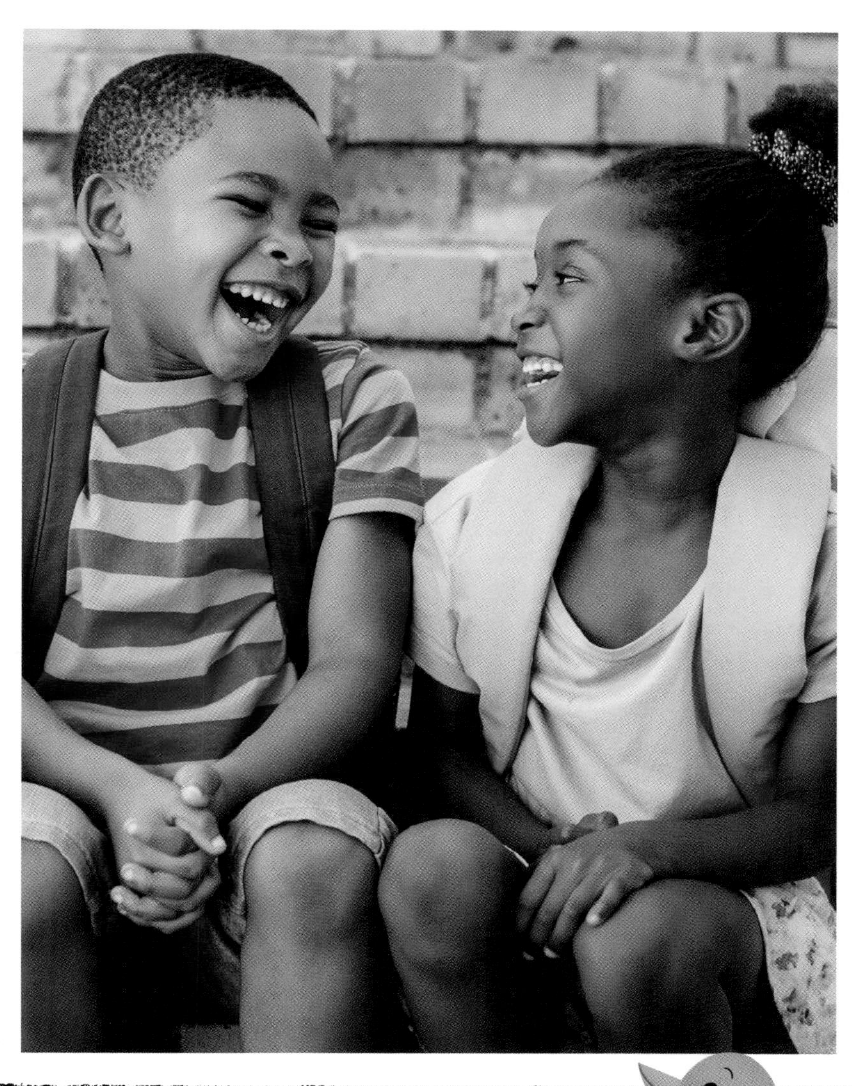

Be sure to listen carefully!

CHAPTER FIVE

Make Choices

Read your notes. Decide what to write in the interview. You don't have to use everything from your notes. Stick with the most interesting points.

ACTIVITY

Writing the Interview

INSTRUCTIONS:

1. Choose the information you want to use from your notes. Put this information into **paragraphs**.
2. Write the interview on another page in your notebook. Imagine you are writing the interview for your classmates to read.
3. Begin by giving the person's name.
4. Write a new paragraph for each **topic**.

AN INTERVIEW WITH THE CHEF AND OWNER OF ROMERO'S

Have you ever eaten at Romero's? If you have, then you know the food is excellent! Lucas Romero is the chef and owner.

Romero was a kid when he came to Dallas, Texas. He came from Mendoza, a city in the mountains of Argentina. His first impression of the United States was how flat it was compared to his other home.

It was hard to make friends at first. So his mother kept him busy helping her in the kitchen. He realized that he liked working in the kitchen and learning how to make dishes from Argentina. As he made friends, he shared his creations.

He is proud of being a citizen of both the United States and Argentina.

CHAPTER SIX

Final Touches

Make your interview report more interesting by adding **quotes**. When you quote someone, you must write exactly what the speaker said. Put quotation marks around the person's words.

ACTIVITY

Quotes

INSTRUCTIONS:

1. Read your interview report.
2. Replay the interview if you used a recording device. Listen for interesting quotes. Make sure you use the person's exact words.
3. Add any quotes to your report using quotation marks.

AN INTERVIEW WITH THE CHEF AND OWNER OF ROMERO'S

Have you ever eaten at Romero's? If you have, then you know the food is excellent! Lucas Romero is the chef and owner.

Romero was a kid when he came to Dallas, Texas. He came from Mendoza, a city in the mountains of Argentina. His first impression of the United States was how flat it was compared to his other home.

It was hard to make friends at first. So his mother kept him busy helping her in the kitchen. He realized that he liked working in the kitchen and learning how to make dishes from Argentina. As he made friends, he shared his creations. "Then I became very popular," said Romero with a laugh.

He is proud of being a citizen of both the United States and Argentina. "I take pride in serving delicious dishes that cross both cultures," he said.

After you finish writing, go over your work. Make changes until everything is just right. Then give the person you interviewed a copy of your writing. Who will you interview next?

GLOSSARY

information (in-fur-MAY-shuhn) knowledge and facts

interview (IN-tur-vyoo) a meeting during which a person is asked questions about themselves or a subject; the report written about this meeting is also called an interview

interviewee (in-tur-vyoo-EE) a person who is being asked questions about themselves or a subject

opinion (uh-PIN-yuhn) a person's beliefs and ideas about somebody or something

paragraphs (PAIR-uh-grafs) groups of sentences about certain ideas or subjects

quotes (KWOHTS) someone's exact words that are copied into a piece of writing

research (REE-surch) careful study of something to learn about it

topic (TAH-pik) the subject of a piece of writing

For More
INFORMATION

BOOKS

Raczka, Bob. *The Vermeer Interviews: Conversations with Seven Works of Art*. Minneapolis, MN: Millbrook Press, 2009.

Truesdell, Ann. *Fire Away: Asking Great Interview Questions*. Ann Arbor, MI: Cherry Lake Publishing, 2013.

WEBSITE

Scholastic—How to Conduct a Journalistic Interview
https://www.scholastic.com/teachers/articles/teaching-content/how-conduct-journalistic-interview
Find more tips for conducting a great interview.

INDEX

About the AUTHORS

Cecilia Minden is the former director of the Language and Literacy Program at Harvard Graduate School of Education. She earned her doctorate from the University of Virginia. Her research focused on early literacy skills and developing phonics curriculums. She is currently a literacy consultant and the author of over 100 books for children. Dr. Minden lives with her family in McKinney, Texas.

Kate Roth has a doctorate from Harvard University in language and literacy and a master's degree from Columbia University Teachers College in curriculum and teaching. Her work focuses on writing instruction in the primary grades. She has taught kindergarten, first grade, and Reading Recovery. She has also instructed hundreds of teachers from around the world in early literacy practices. She lived with her husband and three children in China for many years, and now they live in Connecticut.